Questions You'll Wish You Asked

A TIME CAPSULE JOURNAL FOR
PARENTS AND CHILDREN

Melissa Pennel

Follow Your Fire Publishing
Sacramento, CA.

Melissa Pennel / Follow Your Fire Publishing
FollowYourFireCoaching.com
Sacramento, CA.

Ordering Information:
Quantity sales: Special discounts are available on quantity purchases by corporations, associations, and others. For details, contact the publisher at the address above.

Questions You'll Wish You Asked: A Time Capsule Journal for Parents and Children, Melissa Pennel — 1st ed.

ISBN 978-1-7360095-9-8

This journal belongs to

_____

_____

_____

_____

"You are the bows from which your children
as living arrows are sent forth."

Kahlil Gibran

CONTENTS

Discover more

Questions You'll Wish You Asked

Journals

A Time Capsule Journal for Mothers and Daughters

➹❧

A Time Capsule Journal for Mothers and Sons

➹❧

A Time Capsule Journal for Fathers and Daughters

➹❧

A Time Capsule Journal for Fathers and Sons

➹❧

**A Time Capsule Journal for Grandmothers
and Grandchildren**

➹❧

**A Time Capsule Journal for Grandfathers
and Grandchildren**

➹❧

**A Time Capsule Journal for Grandparents
and Grandchildren**

Learn more at FollowYourFireCoaching.com

For every child asking important questions

&

Every parent brave enough to answer them

Introduction:
A Note to Parents and Children

When my mom (and only parent) died in my late twenties, I felt like I scattered along with her ashes.

Our relationship had been anything but perfect, but it was one I couldn't imagine living without. The bond between parent and child is like that: as ordinary as the familiar silence shared during a car ride, and as profound as the connection one has with their first friend, first teacher, and first love.

Though we talked endlessly in the time we shared on the planet, there were so many questions I had once she left—questions I wish I asked, answers I didn't remember, and information about her that I craved. I was ravenous for her thoughts on love, forgiveness, difficulty, and death; I had so many questions about who she was before me and who she hoped I would become after her.

When I later stumbled upon a journal we had shared, I was blown away. I read and re-read her words, tracing the familiar curve of her handwriting—it felt like I was time travelling, sitting there beside her as she jotted down answers and crossed out mistakes. Though no amount of writing could bring her back to me, this journal has become one of my most treasured possessions: an innocuous item that her death rendered sacred.

Since my mom's unexpected passing, I've often encouraged others to ask their parents questions they might someday have. I believe the benefit is twofold: a deeper understanding of a parent while they're alive, and a legacy to look back on when they're gone.

A mother now myself, I don't know if my kids will crave this information like I did—but just in case they someday do, I created the "Questions You'll Wish You Asked" journal series. I've now witnessed how special the parent/child bond can be...a sacred and foundational relationship that will shape the rest of a child's life.

I created this journal for my children, and I created it for you, too. Though I hope everyone will enjoy and benefit from this book, I wrote it with two groups in mind: children who want to know their parents better, and parents who want to leave a legacy to their children.

Whether bound by blood or any other form of family, I hope these questions open conversations, soften inevitable struggles, and foster moments of intimacy that will be treasured for years to come.

Don't wait to ask these questions or fill out answers; jot some notes down now, and as the years go on feel free to add additional thoughts.

Let these words create an altar where you may visit each other in the future—because however far away it seems now, the time will come for all of us when conversation is no longer possible.

I hope this journal becomes a treasured keepsake that forever reminds you of the sacred and foundational bond that lies between parents and children.

I hope it reminds you of the divine altar you already stand at: that which binds love across time and space.

In love and gratitude,
Melissa Pennel

Your Childhood

What is your earliest memory?

_____

_____

_____

_____

_____

_____

_____

_____

_____

_____

_____

_____

_____

_____

_____

_____

What is a favorite summer memory from childhood?

_____

_____

_____

_____

_____

_____

_____

_____

_____

_____

_____

_____

_____

_____

_____

_____

_____

_____

_____

Did you have any irrational childhood fears?
Do you remember how you got over them?

_____

_____

_____

_____

_____

_____

_____

_____

_____

_____

_____

_____

_____

_____

_____

_____

Did you have a secret hiding place as a child? Where was it?

_____

_____

_____

_____

_____

_____

_____

_____

_____

_____

_____

_____

_____

_____

_____

_____

_____

_____

What is a holiday memory you'll never forget?

_____

_____

_____

_____

_____

_____

_____

_____

_____

_____

_____

_____

_____

_____

_____

_____

What was your favorite game to play as a kid? Why?

_____

_____

_____

_____

_____

_____

_____

_____

_____

_____

_____

_____

_____

_____

_____

_____

_____

What was your favorite childhood meal?

What did you most struggle with as a child?

Who did you look up to as a child?

_____

_____

_____

_____

_____

_____

_____

_____

_____

_____

_____

_____

_____

_____

Did you have a childhood best friend?
What is a dear memory of them?

_____

_____

_____

_____

_____

_____

_____

_____

_____

_____

_____

_____

_____

_____

_____

_____

_____

Did you have childhood pets?
What do you remember about them?

_____

_____

_____

_____

_____

_____

_____

_____

_____

_____

_____

_____

_____

_____

_____

_____

Did you have a favorite toy as a child?
Why was it special?

_____

_____

_____

_____

_____

_____

_____

_____

_____

_____

_____

_____

_____

_____

_____

_____

_____

_____

What were some of your favorite books as a child?

_____

_____

_____

_____

_____

_____

_____

_____

_____

_____

_____

_____

_____

_____

_____

_____

_____

What was a dream you had as a child?

_____

_____

_____

_____

_____

_____

_____

_____

_____

_____

_____

_____

_____

_____

_____

_____

_____

Was there a vacation you took as a child that stands out to you? Why?

**What type of music did your parents listen to?
Did you like it?**

_____

_____

_____

_____

_____

_____

_____

_____

_____

_____

_____

_____

_____

_____

_____

_____

_____

_____

If you could change one thing about your childhood, what would it be?

_____

_____

_____

_____

_____

_____

_____

_____

_____

_____

_____

_____

_____

_____

_____

_____

_____

Did you get along with your siblings?
If an only child, did you ever wish for siblings?

_____

_____

_____

_____

_____

_____

_____

_____

_____

_____

_____

_____

_____

_____

_____

_____

_____

**If you could give your eighteen-year-old self
a piece of advice, what would it be?**

_____

_____

_____

_____

_____

_____

_____

_____

_____

_____

_____

_____

_____

_____

_____

_____

Our Family

What did you learn from your mother?

_____

_____

_____

_____

_____

_____

_____

_____

_____

_____

_____

_____

_____

_____

_____

_____

What did you learn from your father?

What was your favorite thing about your mother?
What about her did you struggle with?

_____

_____

_____

_____

_____

_____

_____

_____

_____

_____

_____

_____

_____

_____

_____

_____

_____

_____

What was your favorite thing about your father?
What about him did you struggle with?

_____

_____

_____

_____

_____

_____

_____

_____

_____

_____

_____

_____

_____

_____

_____

_____

_____

_____

Is there anyone in your family that you wish you'd been closer with?

_____

_____

_____

_____

_____

_____

_____

_____

_____

_____

_____

_____

_____

_____

_____

_____

What are some special memories you have of your grandparents?

_____

_____

_____

_____

_____

_____

_____

_____

_____

_____

_____

_____

_____

_____

_____

_____

_____

Is there any family lore that was passed down to you through stories? Maybe we had a famous ancestor, or mysterious scandal?

_____

_____

_____

_____

_____

_____

_____

_____

_____

_____

_____

_____

_____

_____

_____

_____

_____

**What is something you learned from
the generations before you?**

_____

_____

_____

_____

_____

_____

_____

_____

_____

_____

_____

_____

_____

_____

_____

_____

_____

What was something that your parents found really
important to teach you? Why do you think
it was so important to them?

_____

_____

_____

_____

_____

_____

_____

_____

_____

_____

_____

_____

_____

_____

_____

_____

What did I inherit from your side of the family?

_____

_____

_____

_____

_____

_____

_____

_____

_____

_____

_____

_____

_____

_____

_____

_____

_____

_____

On Parenthood

What are your favorite parts of being a parent?

_____

_____

_____

_____

_____

_____

_____

_____

_____

_____

_____

_____

_____

_____

_____

_____

What is something that has surprised you about parenthood?

How did you choose my name?

_____

_____

_____

_____

_____

_____

_____

_____

_____

_____

_____

_____

_____

_____

_____

_____

What do you remember about our first meeting?

_____

_____

_____

_____

_____

_____

_____

_____

_____

_____

_____

_____

_____

_____

_____

_____

_____

_____

What do you remember about the early days of parenthood?

_____

_____

_____

_____

_____

_____

_____

_____

_____

_____

_____

_____

_____

_____

_____

_____

_____

What was a difficulty of early parenthood?
What did you love about it?

_____

_____

_____

_____

_____

_____

_____

_____

_____

_____

_____

_____

_____

_____

_____

_____

How did becoming a parent change you?

_____

_____

_____

_____

_____

_____

_____

_____

_____

_____

_____

_____

_____

_____

_____

What was I like as a baby, child, teenager?
Was there a point you struggled the most in raising me?

_____

_____

_____

_____

_____

_____

_____

_____

_____

_____

_____

_____

_____

_____

_____

_____

_____

_____

If you could change one thing about how you raised me, what would it be?

_____

_____

_____

_____

_____

_____

_____

_____

_____

_____

_____

_____

_____

_____

_____

_____

What quality do you most hope I inherit from you? Why?

_____

_____

_____

_____

_____

_____

_____

_____

_____

_____

_____

_____

_____

_____

_____

_____

_____

_____

**What is something you hope I *will not*
inherit from you? Why?**

_____

_____

_____

_____

_____

_____

_____

_____

_____

_____

_____

_____

_____

_____

_____

What advice would you give me about raising my own children?

_____

_____

_____

_____

_____

_____

_____

_____

_____

_____

_____

_____

_____

_____

_____

_____

_____

How should I handle judgement from other people?

_____

_____

_____

_____

_____

_____

_____

_____

_____

_____

_____

_____

_____

_____

_____

**What are some things that you hope
I experience in life? Why?**

_____

_____

_____

_____

_____

_____

_____

_____

_____

_____

_____

_____

_____

_____

_____

_____

_____

What is a treasured memory you share of us?

_____

_____

_____

_____

_____

_____

_____

_____

_____

_____

_____

_____

_____

_____

_____

_____

What are you most proud of me for?

If you could make one wish for me, what would it be?

_____

_____

_____

_____

_____

_____

_____

_____

_____

_____

_____

_____

_____

_____

_____

_____

_____

On Work

When asked "what do you want to be when you grow up?" as a child, what did you say?

_____

_____

_____

_____

_____

_____

_____

_____

_____

_____

_____

_____

_____

_____

_____

_____

What was your first job? Did you like it?

_____

_____

_____

_____

_____

_____

_____

_____

_____

_____

_____

_____

_____

_____

_____

_____

_____

_____

_____

What are some ideas you want to pass on to me about work?

_____

_____

_____

_____

_____

_____

_____

_____

_____

_____

_____

_____

_____

_____

_____

_____

_____

Do you love what you do?
Do you think it's important to?

_____

_____

_____

_____

_____

_____

_____

_____

_____

_____

_____

_____

_____

_____

_____

_____

_____

_____

On Love

**Do you remember your first date?
What was it like?**

What advice would you give me about relationships?

_____

_____

_____

_____

_____

_____

_____

_____

_____

_____

_____

_____

_____

_____

_____

_____

What have you learned about yourself from being in love?

_____

_____

_____

_____

_____

_____

_____

_____

_____

_____

_____

_____

_____

_____

_____

_____

What have you learned from heartbreak?

_____

_____

_____

_____

_____

_____

_____

_____

_____

_____

_____

_____

_____

_____

_____

_____

_____

_____

_____

How has your idea of love changed as you've gotten older?

_____

_____

_____

_____

_____

_____

_____

_____

_____

_____

_____

_____

_____

_____

_____

_____

What do you want me to look for in a partner?

_____

_____

_____

_____

_____

_____

_____

_____

_____

_____

_____

_____

_____

_____

_____

_____

Your Spiritual Life

**Did you have a relationship with God or
a Higher Power in childhood?
How did you form it?**

_____

_____

_____

_____

_____

_____

_____

_____

_____

_____

_____

_____

_____

_____

_____

_____

_____

_____

As a child, what was your idea of God?

_____

_____

_____

_____

_____

_____

_____

_____

_____

_____

_____

_____

_____

_____

_____

_____

_____

Today, what is your idea of a Higher Power?

_____

_____

_____

_____

_____

_____

_____

_____

_____

_____

_____

_____

_____

_____

_____

_____

_____

What would you like to teach me about God?

_____

_____

_____

_____

_____

_____

_____

_____

_____

_____

_____

_____

_____

_____

_____

_____

_____

Where do you connect the most with your spirituality?

_____

_____

_____

_____

_____

_____

_____

_____

_____

_____

_____

_____

_____

_____

_____

_____

Knowing You Better

What is a concert you will never forget?
Why was it so memorable?

_____

_____

_____

_____

_____

_____

_____

_____

_____

_____

_____

_____

_____

_____

_____

_____

What is your favorite meal?
What does it remind you of?

_____

_____

_____

_____

_____

_____

_____

_____

_____

_____

_____

_____

_____

_____

_____

_____

_____

What are some of your favorite smells?

_____

_____

_____

_____

_____

_____

_____

_____

_____

_____

_____

_____

_____

_____

_____

What are some of your favorite books?
What do you love about them?

_____

_____

_____

_____

_____

_____

_____

_____

_____

_____

_____

_____

_____

_____

_____

_____

_____

_____

Are there any books you hope I will read? Why?

_____

_____

_____

_____

_____

_____

_____

_____

_____

_____

_____

_____

_____

_____

_____

How do you handle conflict with the people you care about?

_____

_____

_____

_____

_____

_____

_____

_____

_____

_____

_____

_____

_____

_____

_____

_____

_____

_____

What are you insecure about?
Do you know where this came from?

_____

_____

_____

_____

_____

_____

_____

_____

_____

_____

_____

_____

_____

_____

_____

_____

_____

Do you have an embarrassing moment that stands out to you? How did you recover?

_____

_____

_____

_____

_____

_____

_____

_____

_____

_____

_____

_____

_____

_____

_____

_____

_____

What is something you love about yourself?

Is there something that people often get wrong about you?

What is something that always makes you smile?

_____

_____

_____

_____

_____

_____

_____

_____

_____

_____

_____

_____

_____

_____

_____

What have you learned from friendship?

**What is an ordinary moment from your day
that makes you feel extremely grateful?**

_____

_____

_____

_____

_____

_____

_____

_____

_____

_____

_____

_____

_____

_____

_____

_____

Where are your favorite places to travel? Why?

_____

_____

_____

_____

_____

_____

_____

_____

_____

_____

_____

_____

_____

_____

_____

_____

_____

_____

Are there any songs that always make you feel better?

_____

_____

_____

_____

_____

_____

_____

_____

_____

_____

_____

_____

_____

_____

_____

_____

Do you have any favorite quotes?

Life's Tough Moments

**What is one of the toughest decisions
you've ever had to make?**

_____

_____

_____

_____

_____

_____

_____

_____

_____

_____

_____

_____

_____

_____

_____

_____

**What advice would you give me when I am
confused and don't know what path to take?**

_____

_____

_____

_____

_____

_____

_____

_____

_____

_____

_____

_____

_____

_____

_____

_____

What is the first thing you do when you are really afraid?

_____

_____

_____

_____

_____

_____

_____

_____

_____

_____

_____

_____

_____

_____

_____

_____

**What is one of your most difficult experiences?
How did you make it through?**

_____

_____

_____

_____

_____

_____

_____

_____

_____

_____

_____

_____

_____

_____

_____

_____

_____

_____

Was there a particularly challenging phase of your life? How did you cope during that time?

_____

_____

_____

_____

_____

_____

_____

_____

_____

_____

_____

_____

_____

_____

_____

_____

What difficult experience are you now extremely grateful for?

_____

_____

_____

_____

_____

_____

_____

_____

_____

_____

_____

_____

_____

_____

_____

_____

_____

_____

How do you handle major disappointment?

_____

_____

_____

_____

_____

_____

_____

_____

_____

_____

_____

_____

_____

_____

_____

_____

_____

On Saying Goodbye

**What was a difficult goodbye of your life?
How did it change you?**

_____

_____

_____

_____

_____

_____

_____

_____

_____

_____

_____

_____

_____

_____

_____

_____

What do you think happens when we die?
What do you hope happens?

_____

_____

_____

_____

_____

_____

_____

_____

_____

_____

_____

_____

_____

_____

_____

_____

_____

_____

**When you are gone, what is something you will
want me to remember you telling me?**

_____

_____

_____

_____

_____

_____

_____

_____

_____

_____

_____

_____

_____

_____

_____

_____

Is there a tradition of ours that you hope I will continue?
If we don't have any, is there one that you'd like to start?

_____

_____

_____

_____

_____

_____

_____

_____

_____

_____

_____

_____

_____

_____

_____

_____

When you are gone, how do you hope to be remembered?

_____

_____

_____

_____

_____

_____

_____

_____

_____

_____

_____

_____

_____

_____

_____

If you could choose your last words to me, what would they be?

_____

_____

_____

_____

_____

_____

_____

_____

_____

_____

_____

_____

_____

_____

_____

_____

_____

Additional Questions
to Each Other

Use these pages to fill in any additional questions,
answers, or notes to each other

_____

_____

_____

_____

_____

_____

_____

_____

_____

_____

_____

_____

_____

_____

_____

_____

About the Author

Melissa Pennel is a writer, mother, and author of the "Questions You'll Wish You Asked" series of journals. After losing both parents in her twenties, she began urging everyone to ask their parents questions and write down their answers - this journal series was born of that mission.

To find more of Melissa's work on how to live a full and authentic life, go to FollowYourFireCoaching.com.

This journal is in memory of her parents, deLise and Jim.